retired greyhound

understanding and caring for your breed

C000262324

Written by
Julia Barnes

retired greyhound

understanding and
caring for your breed

Written by
Julia Barnes

Pet Book Publishing Company

The Old Hen House St Martin's Farm, Zeals,
Warminster, Wiltshire BA12 6NZ

Printed by Printworks Global Ltd, London & Hong Kong

ISBN:9781-910488-37-9

Acknowledgements

The publishers would like to thank Marcella Zappey for her stunning
photographs.

|Contents

Introducing the Greyhound

One of the most ancient of all breeds, the Greyhound is the fastest dog in the world, and has been honoured throughout time as the supreme canine athlete. But this elegant animal has so much more to offer; he is loving, sweet-tempered and affectionate, making him an ideal companion dog.

The Greyhound is a member of the sighthound family, named for dogs who hunt by sight. Other sighthounds include the Afghan Hound, the Saluki, the Borzoi, and the Whippet, who share the same athletic build – and the same desire to chase.

Physical characteristics

The Greyhound is the supreme racing machine; he can reach speeds of more than 40 miles per hour (64 km per hour) over a distance of half a mile (800

metres). In order to achieve this astonishing feat, he has a unique streamlined physique. From nose to tail tip, he is built for speed, with a frame that allows for a large heart and large lungs which he needs for peak performance.

This is a fine, upstanding dog that has strength and power without a hint of coarseness. He appears angular but his outline is graceful, with a long, narrow head, an elegantly arched neck, and a strong level back. He has a deep chest, long legs and a tail set on low with a slight upwards curve, giving an overall picture of grace and symmetry.

His coat is fine and close-fitting and he comes in a wide variety of colours, with different markings.

Temperament

The Greyhound has a most loving disposition; he is sweet-natured and affectionate and loves to be surrounded by his family. He is gentle with children, and will also suit people who are getting on in years as, contrary to popular opinion, his exercise needs are moderate.

He does enjoy the opportunity to run at full stretch but, more often than not, this takes the form of a 'mad five minutes' when he will sprint round the garden at full tilt, and then just as suddenly, revert to a more sedate pace. A Greyhound's real love is comfort; he may have no equal for speed but he is also in a class of his own when it comes to taking things easy. He is bred to run and chase, but he likes nothing better than lying out, enveloped in cosy bedding, ideally occupying a pool of sunlight.

He is an intelligent dog but like other members of the sighthound family, he is co-operative rather than obedient. He will find his place in the family and will not seek to push the boundaries, which makes him easy to live with, but don't expect a readiness to learn, which you see in other breeds.

A Greyhound is even-tempered, which means that once he is settled in his new home, he will rarely be rattled or stressed. He is peaceable and will get on well with other dogs, especially Greyhounds, but he may have issues with small dogs and cats, which you need to take into consideration if you are planning to adopt an ex-racing Greyhound. See Understanding Greyhounds.

Living with a Greyhound

The Greyhound stands out as the single breed most in need of rehoming. Once his racing career is at an end, he will have many good years ahead of him – but no home to go to.

Dedicated charities work tirelessly to rehome ex-racers – and they do make the most outstanding companions.

However, adopting an adult dog will be a very different experience from taking on a puppy. For those whose circumstances do not allow a puppy, it is an ideal solution. But providing a home for an ex-racing Greyhound will be a voyage of discovery for both of you.

An adult Greyhound comes to you readymade in the sense that he is fully grown – you know exactly what you are getting in terms of size and appearance.

He will also have developed his own personality and although this may change, and hopefully blossom in a home setting, he will have his own back story which will influence his behaviour.

An ex-racing Greyhound will have spent his life in kennels so he will take time to adapt to his new home. You need to be patient with him as he learns the house rules, and becomes acquainted with a world that is far removed from the racing kennels and the track.

That said, a Greyhound loves his creature comforts and it will not be long before he is lapping up the luxury of living in a family home.

Facing page: The Greyhound quickly becomes a convert to easy living...

Tracing back in time

The Greyhound is thought to be the earliest purebred breed in existence with a history dating back some 8,000 years.

Drawings of Greyhound-like dogs were discovered in the ancient Turkish town of Catel-Huyuk, and have been dated around 600BC. They show dogs in pursuit of a stag, with narrow heads, long legs, deep chests and powerful hindquarters. Other proof of the Greyhound's ancient history comes from images found on a vase in south-west Iran, dated 4200 BC, and sketches discovered in the Algerian Sahara going back to 3000 BC. Over the following five centuries the breed made its way to Egypt.

Hunting dogs

The Egyptians were great dog lovers, and the Greyhound, with his elegant appearance and hunting prowess soon became a great favourite. Hunting was a popular pastime; the method employed was to release two Greyhounds to chase, bring down and kill they prey which included hares, antelopes, gazelles, stags and even ostriches.

A high value was placed on the best Greyhounds; they were given as gifts to foreign dignitaries and used as barter for goods and services. In this way, the Greyhound made its way to the Middle East and further afield.

The Greeks were as keen on the new breed as the Egyptians and there are numerous depictions of Greyhounds on pottery, jewellery and on coins, dating back to 1000 BC. In 800 BC, Homer, the Greek poet, describes a Greyhound called Argos in The Odyssey – he was the only one to recognise his returning master, Odysseus, after a long absence.

The Greyhound enjoyed an honoured place throughout the Roman Empire where he was given a dual role as hunting dog and family companion. However, the fall of the Roman Empire in AD 476 led to the destruction of thousands of Greyhounds who had travelled with the Roman armies.

The Greyhound survived, thanks to the intervention of the Irish clergy. Priests realised they could make good money by breeding hunting dogs for the aristocracy, and thus saved the breed from extinction.

Gradually, the Greyhound was established throughout Europe as a a supreme hunting and coursing dog. The breed was the preserve of the nobility, and many Royal households were proud of their teams of Greyhounds.

The elegant Greyhound was the the breed of choice in royal households.

Developing the breed

Many dog breeds were developed for hunting, and over the course of history their role became redundant. Not so the Greyhound. His talents were put to a new use – chasing an artificial lure.

Coursing became the sport of choice in both the UK and the USA, and Greyhounds were unleashed to pursue hares and jack rabbits. But in 1912, a new invention revolutionised the lives of Greyhounds.

An American, named Patrick Owen Smith, invented a mechanical lure that could travel round an oval circuit. The first Greyhound track was opened in Emeryville, California in 1919, and after a slow start the new sport took off.

The introduction of floodlights was significant as this enabled enthusiasts to go racing and wage bets after they had finished work.

The sport spread to Britain, and under the auspices of the Greyhound Racing Association, the first track was opened at Belle Vue, Manchester.

A crowd of 1,700 witnessed the first meeting on July 24th 1926, where six races were staged over a course of 440 yards. The distinction of winning the first race on British soil went to a Greyhound called Mistley.

Greyhound racing thrived, helped by some exceptional performers such as Mick The Miler, who became so famous that he starred in a film called Wild Boy in 1935. In its heyday in the 1950s and 1960s crowds in excess of 60,000 turned up to watch the major competitions.

The modern era

On both sides of the Atlantic, and in Australia, Greyhound racing continues but in a much reduced form. The scarcity of land and the push for building housing and retail outlets has led to the closure of many tracks, and it is now very much a minority sport.

However, while Greyhound racing continues, breeders will produce dogs for the track, who need rehoming once their careers come to an end.

So, the need to adopt ex-racers remains paramount – and the dedicated owners who take up this option will be rewarded by a fantastic canine companion.

What should a Greyhound look like?

The Greyhound is the supreme racing machine and the demands of pace, power and acceleration dictate his appearance. The result is one of the most elegant of breeds – so how is a Greyhound put together?

The aim of breeders is to produce dogs that are sound healthy, typical examples of their chosen breed, in terms of both looks and temperament. To achieve this, they are guided by a Breed Standard, which is a written blueprint describing the perfect specimen.

In the show ring, judges use the Breed Standard to assess the dogs that come before them, and it is the dog that, in their opinion, comes closest to the

ideal, that will win top honours.

This has significance beyond the sport of showing, for it is the dogs that win in the ring which will be used for breeding. The winners of today are therefore responsible for passing on their genes to future generations and preserving the breed in its best form.

In the world of racing Greyhounds, appearance is not a top priority – it is all about speed. It is, therefore, the top performers on the track that will be used for breeding. However, a Greyhound can only run at speed if he has the conformation and the physique that equips him for this demanding role.

Greyhounds have been developed over many centuries to be the fastest of all breeds, and the Breed Standard of today reflects this, giving a picture in words of what this canine racing machine should look like.

There are some differences between Greyhounds that are bred for the show ring and racing Greyhounds; the show Greyhound is a taller, more substantial animal. However, it is interesting to look at the Breed Standard in some detail in order to understand how the breed has been fine-tuned to be strong, powerful and fleet of foot.

Breed Standards may vary slightly depending on the governing body. In the case of the Greyhound, there is some discrepancy on the issue of size.

The American Kennel Club (AKC) also gives a scale of points, which indicates the value that is given to various physical attributes.

AKC Scale of points

General symmetry and quality	10
Head and neck	20
Chest and shoulders	20
Back	10
Quarters	20
Legs and feet	20
Total	100

General appearance

The Greyhound is strongly built; his muscular appearance gives an impression of an upstanding animal of generous proportions.

He appears symmetrical with flowing, athletic lines which denote both elegance and power.

Temperament

The typical Greyhound temperament is gentle and affectionate. He is intelligent, but perhaps more importantly, he is even-tempered which makes him an outstanding companion dog.

Head

The Greyhound's streamlined appearance starts with his head, which is long, moderate in width, with a flat skull. The stop, the step-up between the muzzle and the forehead, is slight.

The muzzle should be of good length and should appear powerful without being coarse. The jaws are well chiselled.

Eyes

The eyes are oval in shape and are set obliquely. Regardless of coat colour, the eyes should be dark with a bright, intelligent expression indicating the spirit of the breed.

Ears

The Greyhound's ears are small and rose-shaped. They are fine in texture and are thrown back and folded unless the dog is alert, when they are semi-pricked. Some racing Greyhounds have erect ears, but this is frowned upon in the show ring.

Mouth

The jaws are strong and the teeth meet in a perfect scissor bite with the teeth on the upper jaw closely overlapping the teeth on the lower jaw.

Neck

The neck is long and muscular. It is elegantly arched as is widens gradually into the shoulders. There should be no hint of throatiness.

This is a breed that is built for action.

Forequarters

The lay of the shoulders is extremely important for a dog that is built to cover the ground and move at speed. The shoulders are placed obliquely and are muscular without being loaded. They are cleanly defined at the top. The forelegs are long and straight, and should show substance and quality. The elbows are set under the shoulders and the pasterns are slightly sprung and of moderate length.

Body

A deep chest is a feature of the breed, providing plenty of room for the heart and lungs. The Breed Standard states that the chest falls level with the elbows; the ribcage is also deep and the ribs are well sprung. The back is long, broad and square; the loins are muscular, powerful and slightly arched.

Hindquarters

The hindquarters are the powerhouse, and the rear end of a Greyhound should be designed with ample proportions. The thighs and second thighs are wide and muscular with great powers of propulsion; the stifles (knee joints) are well bent and the hocks (ankles) are well let down, turning neither inwards nor outwards. When viewed from the rear, there is an appearance of perfect symmetry.

Facing page: The typical free-reaching stride of a Greyhound.

Feet

The feet are more hare-like than cat-like; they are compact, well knuckled up with good, strong claws.

Tail

Set on rather low, the tail is long, strong at the root and tapers to a fine point. It is carried low and has a slight upward curve.

Coat

The Greyhound has a short, smooth, fine coat, which lies close to the body and has a firm texture.

Colour

This is a breed that comes in a wide variety of colours and markings. Greyhounds may be white, black, red, blue, fawn or brindle.

They may have white markings or any of the colours may be broken with white.

Movement

If a Greyhound is built correctly, he will move correctly. Typically, he has a low-reaching, free stride which allows him to cover the ground at great speed. When galloping his hind legs come well under the body giving great propulsion.

Size

The Breed Standard in the UK states that males should be 71-76cm (28-30in) in height, females should be 69-71cm (27-28in).

The American Breed Standard does not give any guidance on height but states that males should weigh 65-70lb (27-30kg) and females should be 60-65lb (30-32kg)

Summing up

The majority of Greyhounds that are kept as pet dogs are ex-racers and those that breed racing dogs are concerned with pace rather than appearance.

However, the health of the breed is a top priority regardless of whether you are racing or showing your dog, or whether you are simply keeping him as a pet.

A Breed Standard ensures that exaggeration does not creep in and that Greyhounds remain sound in mind and body, and retain the characteristics that are unique to this very special breed.

Understanding Greyhounds

There are over 200 dog breeds to choose from, so how can you be sure that the Greyhound is the right breed for you? Before you decide to take on an ex-racer you need to be 100 per cent confident that you can cope with a dog that has spent the first years of his life in kennels.

Racing Greyhounds have limited experience of the outside world and so it helps if you know something of their background story. During the course of their racing lives, they will have acquired some social skills – but they may not be what you expect.

Early lives

Greyhound are bred specifically for the track, using males and females that have had enjoyed successful racing careers. In many cases, stud dogs command high fees for their services.

Generally, puppies are born in kennels, and will be cared for by the breeder and kennel staff, so they will be used to interacting with people from an early age. They will be fed communally once they are weaned, and will be kept together as a litter.

For the first 12 months of their lives, the puppies are given as much freedom as possible so they grow in strength both physically and mentally. They will spend much of the day free exercising in large grass paddocks, although they will be checked over and handled on a regular basis,

At 12 months of age, they will start to be schooled behind an artificial lure. The breeder may undertake this task, or some youngsters may be taken on by Greyhound trainers at this stage. The Greyhound is first hand-slipped behind the lure and then he learns to use a starting trap. Initially, he will be trained on a straight, and graduate to running around an oval track. Once he has proved that he can chase a lure without interfering with other Greyhounds, and is bold enough to take the lead rather than run alongside the other dogs, he is ready for the track.

Racing dogs

Greyhound trainers have their own ways of doing things but the majority of racing Greyhounds will be accustomed to the following routine.

The day starts with kennel cleaning and the Greyhounds, who are usually kennelled in pairs, are let out into concrete runs. A light cereal breakfast is served and the morning is spent exercising the dogs and grooming them.

Each Greyhound will be given a thorough grooming which includes teeth-cleaning and nail trimming. He will be give a massage, which is a hands on experience used to tone the muscles.

He will then be given any medical treatment that is necessary. Greyhounds can get injured on the track, and as the stakes are high for a successful dog, all the most up to date therapies are employed to get a dog back to race fitness. This may include ultrasound, acupuncture or hydrotherapy.

Exercise is divided between lead walking and free running. Greyhounds are generally walked in pairs, and they will be taken around the trainer's premises or maybe on public footpaths, so they have some, albeit limited, experience of the outside world.

Greyhounds are turned out in extensive grass paddocks for free running exercise. Gallops may be used if a Greyhound is preparing for a big competition or is returning to race fitness after a rest or following an injury.

The main meal is fed in the early afternoon, and the rest of the day is spent alternating Greyhounds in the exercise paddocks and preparing dogs that are due to race that evening. On race days, Greyhounds are fed a light lunch and will have the rest of their rations after racing.

They travel to the track in a purpose built Greyhound carrier, fitted with crates, or if there is only one or two dogs travelling to a big competition further afield, they will travel in an estate car or a van, again fitted with crates. At the track, the Greyhound will be kennelled prior to racing and will then be paraded around the track. At the start of the race they are put into starting traps and then caught once they have crossed the finishing line.

Facing page: Trainers pay great attention to detail to get the best from the Greyhounds in their care.

What your Greyhound knows

Following his life as a racing dog your Greyhound will have learnt:

- How to interact with people, although generally this will be adults only.

- How to cope with being handled, which includes grooming, routine health care, veterinary examinations and treatments.

- How to live with other Greyhounds.

- How to walk on the lead.

- How to cope with time alone (or solely in the company of a kennel-mate).

- How to travel.

What your Greyhound doesn't know

There will be many blanks in your Greyhound's education. He will not know:

- How to live in a house.

- How to interact with children.

- How to live with cats and other small animals (an unrealistic expectation for most Greyhounds).

- How to meet and greet dogs other than Greyhounds.

- How to cope with being walked in a busy built-up area.

There will be significant gaps in your Greyhound's education

So you can see that if you take on an ex-racer you will have just as much work to do as if you were bringing a puppy into your home.

However, if you progress at a pace that your Greyhound feels comfortable with, he will start to trust you. This means that he will take the lead from you and will be able to cope with situations he has not encountered before.

What can you expect from your Greyhound?

If you are taking on an ex-racer, you need to be fully aware that this is a breed with a strong prey drive – he would not have the motivation to follow an artificial lure unless he was hard-wired to sighting prey and giving chase.

As the name implies, a sighthound hunts by sight, and his instinctive urge to run down prey is triggered by movement.

This behaviour is highly desirable in a hunting dog, and it has been adapted to the sport of racing, but it is not so useful when it is directed towards cats and other small animals a companion Greyhound may come across in his new home. As with all animals and

people, the Greyhound is very much an individual and not every dog is preoccupied with chasing small, furry animals. There are three main categories to consider when deciding whether you can take on an ex-racer:

Non-chasers

Firstly, there are those Greyhounds who have been bred to race and have been schooled for the track, but show no interest in following the artificial lure. These non-chasers make ideal companions and will still be relatively young as, clearly, they have no future as racing dogs.

In most cases, their prey instinct is dulled to the extent that they can be trained to live alongside the family cat. However, never say never: all dogs, regardless of breed, can suddenly be stimulated by something that moves, and a degree of vigilance will always be required

Curtailed career

The second category of ex-racers are those that have put the past behind them and, with it, the desire to chase. This type of Greyhound may have got as far as the track but lacked the keenness and drive to be a contender. He may have preferred to run with the other Greyhounds rather than forging ahead, or he may have been too slow and unmotivated to make the grade.

If a racing dog is failing in this way, he will be retired early, probably when he is around two to three years of age. As the chasing instinct is diluted, these dogs will adapt well to a family situation and may be trained to live alongside cats and other small animals.

Some Greyhounds have a very low prey drive, but they are in the minority.

However, you should always remain cautious as if something suddenly triggers a chase response, a Greyhound will not be able to control himself. He will be beyond the reach of rational thought – and the consequences could be disastrous.

Fully fledged racing dogs

The third category of ex-racers are those that have had a full career as racing dogs. In most cases, a Greyhound will be retired when he is four or five years of age unless his career has been cut short by injury.

The majority of these dogs will have a strong chasing instinct which has become ingrained through use.

They will adapt to living in a home and make excellent companions, but you need to accept that your dog may need to be muzzled when he is out in public places and his free running opportunities will be severely limited.

This may sound like a drawback, but it should be viewed as a different experience of dog ownership.

An ex-racing Greyhound will enjoy the freedom of his home and garden and will be perfectly happy to be exercised on-lead as long as he has the opportunity to explore new places, with the occasional bonus of a free run when you are in a safe and suitable environment.

Facing page: Living with an ex-racer requires some adjustments on both sides...

What can your Greyhound expect from you?

A dog cannot speak for himself, so we need to view the world from a canine perspective and work out what a Greyhound needs in order to live a happy, contented and fulfilling life.

Time and commitment

First of all, a Greyhound needs a commitment that you will care for him for the duration of his life, guiding him through the period when he is adapting to a new home, enjoying his companionship as he becomes settled, and being there for him in his later years.

The Greyhound was bred for his extraordinary speed but he has other, outstanding talents. His ability to adapt from racing dog to companion dog is truly

remarkable – all he needs is a little help and support from you.

You need to take charge of his education so that he understands his place in the family and has the confidence to live in the wider community. You will need to spend time socialising him so that he learns to take all new situations in his stride.

You also need to bear in mind that your Greyhound is no longer a kennel dog. He may have spent long periods in this environment but, invariably, he would have the companionship of other dogs. If he is rehomed as a single dog, he will have to adapt to this major change.

He needs to become part of the family and be included in family activities. If he is expected to spend lengthy periods on his own, he will not only be thoroughly miserable, he may well invent his own agenda and spend the time barking and whining or being destructive.

It is important that all dogs can cope with spending some time on their own so they don't become anxious, but the maximum time a dog should be left is four hours.

If this does not fit in with your lifestyle, you should delay owning a dog until your circumstances change.

Practical matters

The Greyhound is a low maintenance dog when it comes to looking after him. In terms of coat care, he needs minimal grooming and as long as your pursue a programme of routine preventative care, he is hardy and healthy.

With regards to exercise, the Greyhound is quite a surprise. Many people think this canine athlete will need huge amounts of strenuous exercise but this is simply not the case. A Greyhound will enjoy pottering about and he will thrive on the mental stimulation of going to new places, but that will be sufficient. If it's raining, he may think twice about venturing out at all!

You need to introduce your Greyhound to his new life as a family pet.

Leadership

The Greyhound is not a pushy breed; he feels no real need to exert his authority and he will be content with his place in the family circle.

However, he has a lot to learn as he undergoes the transformation from racing dog to companion dog.

It is your job to show your Greyhound how you want him to behave by rewarding the behaviour that you consider desirable. You need to be 100 per cent consistent so he is left in no doubt as to what you want – and what you don't want.

If he gets it 'wrong' do not tell him off as he will be confused and lose confidence. Simply interrupt his behaviour by refocusing his attention using a tasty treat.

As soon as he makes the 'right' decision and changes his behaviour, you can reward him handsomely.

In this way, your Greyhound learns good manners without the need for force or coercion. He is living with you in peace and harmony because he understands what you want him to do, and he respects you.

Facing page:
Consistency is the key
to successful training.

Adopting a Greyhound

> Now you have decided that you want to go ahead and adopt a Greyhound, how should you go about it?

There are a wide variety of organisations that specialise in rehoming ex-racing Greyhounds ranging from small set-ups which are run entirely by volunteers to much bigger operations which are part-funded by the racing industry.

In the UK, the Retired Greyhound Trust (RGT) has a network of more than 70 affiliated bodies and branches, making it the biggest single breed charity in the country. It finds homes for over 4,000 Greyhounds every year.

There are many other similar organisations that work independently of the RGT, striving to find homes for all the Greyhounds that have to come to the end of their racing careers.

Some charities do not have kennelling facilities but instead rely on foster carers, who look after ex-racers in their own homes prior to adoption. Details of these charities may be found on the Internet, or by using local contacts such as veterinary surgeries which will have information on what is going on in your area.

In the USA, there are a number of organisations devoted to rehoming ex-racers – the National Greyhound Adoption Program (NGAP) being the best known. This is based in Philadelphia, and ex-racers from all over the USA are transported to the centre for rehoming. It has top-class facilities, including kennelling for 50 Greyhounds, indoor and outdoor runs and a state of the art veterinary clinic. Again there are a number of smaller rehoming charities which operate on a local or regional basis.

Both the larger national charities – the Retired Greyhound Trust and the National Greyhound Adoption Program – have excellent websites which give invaluable information on ex-racers, as well as describing the work they do and the Greyhounds that are available for adoption.

Rehoming procedures vary depending on the rehoming organisations, but they follow a broadly similar format.

First visit

You may have already contacted the rehoming charity and filled in preliminary forms which will give some indication of the home you can offer and the type of Greyhound you are looking for.

But you will find out a lot more when you first visit

the rehoming centre. Not only will you see lots of different Greyhounds, you will have the opportunity to become better acquainted with the adoption process.

If you are planning to adopt, you will be asked lots of questions about your home, your family, and your lifestyle. Bear in mind, the staff are not being invasive; the aim is to find a home where a Greyhound can thrive, avoiding all possible pitfalls.

You will be asked some or all of the following questions:

- What is your home set up?

- Do you have children/grandchildren?

- What are their ages?

- Do you have a securely-fenced garden?

- Is there somebody at home the majority of the time?

- What is your previous experience with dogs?

- Do you already have a dog at home? If so, what breed or size is he?

- Do you have a cat?

- Where do you plan to exercise your Greyhound?

Home check

Once you made your choice, rehoming staff will organise a home check to see if you have the facilities to care for a Greyhound (see A Greyhound Friendly Home). In the meantime, you will be allowed to visit your prospective pet so you can get to know each other. You will be able to take him for walks (on lead) at the rehoming centre, and he will be able to meet all members of his future family.

A free exchange of information between rehoming staff and prospective owners is essential.

Following the home check, you will get the go ahead to officially adopt your Greyhound. The Retired Greyhound Trust in the UK asks for a a fee to cover vaccinations, neutering preventative worming and flea treatment. The National Greyhound Adoption Program in the U.S also asks for a set fee which covers all of the above plus heartworm and thyroid testing, and dental cleaning.

Once you have handed over the money and completed the relevant paperwork, you will be ready to take your Greyhound home and start your new life together.

The right choice

When you visit a rehoming centre and look at the Greyhounds who are up for adoption, you will feel like taking the whole lot home with you! However, this is a situation when you must not allow your heart to rule your head. It is vitally important for both you, and the dog you adopt, to make the right choice. You want to give a Greyhound a forever home, and this will only happen if you find a dog that will fit in with your home, your family and your lifestyle.

Building a profile

Staff at rehoming centres find out as much about individual Greyhounds as possible, and this

All Greyhounds have their own individual personalities so you need help to find a dog that will fit in with your family.

background information is crucial when it comes to making the right choice.

A Greyhound will be tested to assess his general temperament – whether he is a bold, out-going character who will cope with the hurly burly of a busy household or whether he is more withdrawn – perhaps a little nervous – and would suit a quieter home.

He will be assessed for his compatability with children of different ages, and he will also be tested to see if he can live with small dogs, which can trigger his prey drive.

In some rehoming centres, they have a resident cat, so a Greyhound's reaction to small, furry animals can be checked out.

A typical profile would be:

Name: Blaze

DOB: 22/7/2012

Gender: Male

Colour: Black and white

Blaze is one of our older Greyhounds who is looking for a forever home. He is a calm, laid-back individual who gets on with children of all ages.

He travels well and loves his cuddles. He is very sociable with people and likes to explore his environment.

However, he is not small dog friendly. Blaze would do best in a home living as a solo dog or with another Greyhound. When he is exercised outside the home, he will need to be muzzled and walked on-lead.

The rehoming staff are at pains to paint an accurate picture in order to make the best possible match. In return, you need to be completely honest about the home you can offer. It may be that a number of Greyhounds will rule themselves out because they will not fit in with your family or your lifestyle, and this will help to narrow your choice. There are a number of other factors to consider when selecting an ex-racing Greyhound:

Male or female?

The choice of male or female Greyhound comes down to personal preference. Males are harder to rehome than females, and this is generally the result of misconceptions:

- Males are bigger and stronger and are therefore harder to handle

It is certainly true that a male is bigger, but this does not mean he is going to use his strength to tow you around. A compact female can be a veritable powerhouse and could just as easily cause problems if she is not properly lead-trained.

- Males have a more highly developed prey drive

Not true. The chase instinct is equally strong in both sexes. You need to assess the individual dog to evaluate this aspect of their temperament.

- Males that have been kept entire during their racing career will be over-sexed

All Greyhounds are neutered before rehoming and this will, obviously, have a major effect on hormonal activity. It is rare for overtly 'male' behaviour to cause problems but, again, every dog is an individual and should be assessed accordingly.

- Males are not as affectionate as females

All Greyhounds have a gentle, loving disposition regardless of gender. Some may be more aloof than others, some may be softer than others – but this applies equally to males and females.

So, in reality, there is nothing to choose between males and females. Of course, you must follow your own preference but if you are undecided, think about taking on a male. The boys are so much harder to rehome, simply as a result of misunderstanding...

Facing page: Preconceived notions about gender are not always accurate.

Colour

There are lots of colours and markings to choose from, and you may have a favourite. There is no doubt that appearance plays a part when people are choosing which Greyhound they want to adopt, and the dog's colour and markings come into play. In terms of popularity, blue Greyhounds are snapped up quickly, but there are so many lovely colours and colour combinations to choose from, you will probably be spoilt for choice.

Age

If you have decided to adopt an ex-racer, you will be taking on a mature, adult dog. As already highlighted, the age at which a Greyhound will be retired from the track will vary from as young as two years old to around five years of age. If a Greyhound has been in the rehoming centre for some time, he may be older.

The age of your prospective Greyhound may seem significant but, in fact, his past history is far more relevant as this will have influenced his character and his current behaviour.

It is therefore best to look at the dog that will fit in with your lifestyle rather than being preoccupied with his age.

More than one?

Greyhounds are highly collectable, and they really do enjoy each other's company. However, do not be in too much of a hurry to add to your Greyhound population. An ex-racer may take some time to find his feet in his new home and you want to ensure that he is well established before you take on a second dog.

In racing kennels, Greyhounds are generally kennelled in male/female pairs. This combination will work equally well in a domestic setting, particularly as all ex-racers are neutered before rehoming.

However, there are some Greyhounds who do not relish canine companionship; they are in the minority but they do exist. It is therefore very important that you find out about this aspect of a Greyhound's temperament before making the decision to take on a second dog.

Wait until your first Greyhound is established in his new home before taking on a companion for him.

A Greyhound friendly home

When you adopt an ex-racer, he will have to adapt from a lifetime of living in kennels to becoming a house pet. The Greyhound loves his creature comforts, so he will be only too happy to make the transition. However, you need to make sure your home is safe and secure as he will be in an entirely new environment.

In the home

Bringing an adult dog into your home is an entirely different matter to taking on a puppy. A fully grown Greyhound will not be so playful, which means he will not get into mischief so easily, but there will probably be some changes you need to make.

Try to see the house from a Greyhound's perspective and this will enable you to spot potential trouble-spots.

Flooring can be an area of concern as a Greyhound that is used to kennel life will not be used to negotiating tiles, wooden flooring or linoleum, which can be very slippery.

You do not want to cause your Greyhound unnecessary anxiety as he gets used to his new home so think about buying some mats and placing then strategically so your dog can pick his route.

Your Greyhound is highly unlikely to cause problems with chewing in the way that a puppy would, but there is something else to bear in mind. A Greyhound is the ideal height for reaching table-tops and kitchen work surfaces, so you need to keep them free from edible substances.

A Greyhound, fresh from kennels, will have never been in a kitchen before and he will be entranced by what appears to be on offer. He will have no concept that stealing is 'wrong' and so it is better to keep temptation at bay.

You may decide to declare upstairs off-limits; the best way of doing this is to install a baby gate; these can also be useful if you want to limit your

Greyhound's freedom in any other part of the house. This barrier works well as your dog is separate but does not feel excluded from what is going on.

In the garden

Greyhounds are not born escapists but they have the ability to overcome obstacles and make a break for freedom if the mood takes them. For this reason, your garden will need to be securely fenced; a height of 1.5 metres (5ft) is a minimum requirement. If you have gates leading out of your property, they must have secure fastenings.

If you are a keen gardener, you may want to think about creating an area of garden that is free from plants and shrubs that can be used for toileting. This helps the house-training process and makes cleaning up easier.

If you allow your Greyhound free access to the garden you should be aware that there are a number of plants that are toxic to dogs, such as tulip bulbs, lily of the valley, azaleas, jasmine and daffodil flowers. You can find a comprehensive list on the Internet. You also need to be aware that garden chemicals, such as fertilisers, fungicides and pesticides, are highly toxic so be very careful where you use them.

House rules

Before your Greyhound comes home, hold a family conference to work out the house rules. You need to decide which rooms your Greyhound will have access to and also decide whether he is to be allowed on the furniture or not.

It is important to start as you mean to go on. You cannot invite your dog on to the sofa for cuddles when he is clean and dry and then reprimand him when he climbs up after a muddy walk.

A Greyhound has so much to get used to as he acclimatises to life in a home you need to help him as much as possible.

This means giving clear messages, and being 100 per cent consistent so that he understands what is the 'correct' behaviour in an environment that he will find completely baffling until he finds his feet.

Buying equipment

There are some essential items of equipment you will need for your Greyhound. If you choose wisely, much of it will last for many years to come. Some of the bigger rehoming charities have shops that specialise in Greyhound supplies.

If you buy from them you will not only get products that have been tried and tested on Greyhounds, you will also be helping the rehoming charity.

Indoor crate

An ex-racing Greyhound is used to living in a kennel, which is his own special place where he can rest undisturbed. It is therefore useful to recreate a den-like space in the home where he can feel safe and secure.

An indoor crate is the ideal way of doing this, and when it is lined with soft bedding your Greyhound can use it at will.

Look at your home from a Greyhound's perspective.

When you leave your Greyhound, either overnight or when you go out during the day, he can settle in his crate which will minimise any feelings of anxiety he may have. The ideal size for an adult Greyhound is 122cm x 91cm (48 x 36in).

You will also need to consider where you are going to locate the crate. The kitchen is usually the most suitable place as this is the hub of family life. Try to find a snug corner, free from draughts, where your Greyhound can rest when he wants to but where he can also see what is going on around him, and still be with the family.

Beds and bedding

The crate will need to be lined with bedding. A heavy-duty waterproof mattress is ideal and it provides sufficient depth to preclude pressure points on the dog's body which can cause discomfort and partial baldness.

If you have purchased a crate, you may not feel the need to buy an extra bed, although your Greyhound may like to have a bed in the family room so he feels part of household activities.

There is an amazing array of dog-beds to chose from – duvets, bean bags, cushions, baskets, igloos, mini-four posters – but you need to consider a

Facing page: Cosy bedding is a must for this thin-skinned breed.

Greyhound's size and conformation. It is important that the sides of the bed are firm and stay upright when they are put under pressure, and it needs to be big enough to accommodate a Greyhound when he is lying on his side.

If you want to provide some extra bedding, a duvet is always much appreciated by a Greyhound as it provides ample cushioning when it is folded over.

Collar and lead

A conventional dog collar will not be suitable for a Greyhound; his neck is bigger and wider than his head and so it is an easy matter for him to back out and escape. The best type of collar is the martingale type which can be left on the dog and used as a house collar.

For outside wear, a good-quality, leather fishtail collar works best. The fishtail design widens to approximately 6.35cm (2.5in) at its widest point which ensures maximum comfort and security.

A leather lead is kind to your hands, which is important when you consider how much lead-walking you will do with your Greyhound. Make sure it has a secure trigger fastening.

The length of lead is a matter of personal preference; a longer lead – 122cm (48in) – allows your Greyhound more freedom if he is trained to walk on a loose lead, but if you are in a built-up area a shorter lead is preferable,

You may consider buying an extending lead which allows your Greyhound to roam at a short distance from you. However, it is not always easy to control a Greyhound in this situation so unless your dog is very placid, it may be more trouble than it is worth.

If you decide an extending lead is suitable, never use it when you are walking in built up areas. An unexpected lunge from your Greyhound could take him on to the road with potentially disastrous consequences.

Harness

You may prefer walking your Greyhound in a harness, which allows a little more freedom and may be more comfortable. However, an ex-racer will not be used to this type of equipment so you will need to introduce it tactfully – maybe give him a few weeks to settle before trying it.

There are a variety of different designs on the market, and you will need to find the type that suits your dog. A harness made from polar fleece generally works well as it is soft on the skin and chafing is reduced to a minimum.

Muzzle

A racing Greyhound wears a lightweight muzzle when he is on the track, and so he is entirely accustomed to wearing this piece of equipment. Owners of retired Greyhounds generally opt for a plastic muzzle which is durable and more practical for everyday use. It is essential in the early days of rehoming when you may be introducing your Greyhound to family pets, and it can be useful when you are carrying out routine tasks, such as nail trimming, until your Greyhound is more relaxed.

Depending on your Greyhound's temperament and prey drive, it may be advisable for him to wear a muzzle in public places. The rehoming charity will advise you on this. Bear in mind, a muzzle is used purely as a precaution, it does not mean that your Greyhound is aggressive.

ID

Your Greyhound needs to wear some form of ID when he is out in public places. An ex-racer will have his registration number tattooed on the inside of his ears, but he now needs ID for a pet dog living in the community. This can be in the form of a disc, engraved with your contact details, attached to the collar.

Microchipping, which is a permanent form of ID, is now a legal requirement in the UK. A microchip is the size of a grain of rice. It is injected under the skin, usually between the shoulder blades, with a special needle. It has tiny barbs on it, which dig into the tissue around where it lies, so it does not migrate from that spot.

Each chip has its own unique identification number which can only be read by a special scanner. That ID number is then registered on a national database with your name and details, so that if ever your dog is lost, he can be taken to any vet or rescue centre where he is scanned and then you are contacted. A number of rehoming charities are now providing microchipping as part of their rehoming service.

Your Greyhound needs to wear an ID tag when he is in public places.

Walking out coat

Greyhounds carry very little body fat and will therefore feel the cold. There are lots of different walking out coats to choose from, and you can build up an entire wardrobe to cater for all weathers! As a minimum you will need a waterproof jacket, ideally fleece-lined.

Bowls

A Greyhound is a tall dog and therefore he has to stretch down to reach a bowl that is at floor level. This is not ideal for a number of reasons:

Over a period of time, stretching down imposes strain on the neck, shoulder and back muscles and puts pressure on the joints.

Digestion may be impaired by feeding in an awkward position which can lead to flatulence and/or constipation. In a worst case scenario, it could increase the risk of bloating. This is a life-threatening condition where the gut fills with gas and air and then twists; it can only be resolved with emergency surgery.

A Greyhound will make a lot more mess when he is eating or drinking from a bowl at floor level.

The solution is to buy a feeding stand, which raises the bowl to a level where it is easy to access. You can

Facing page:
Greyhounds do
feel the cold.

buy a double feeding stand, with one bowl for food and the other for water.

Food

The rehoming charity will let you know what your Greyhound is eating and should provide a comprehensive diet sheet. It is a good idea to get a supply of this food so you do not have to introduce a change of diet while your Greyhound is settling in his new home.

For more information on feeding, see Choosing a diet.

Grooming gear

The Greyhound is a low maintenance breed in terms of coat care but there are a few essentials you will need:

- Body brush – for removing dirt and debris from the coat.

- Rubber grooming mitt – acts as a massage and improves circulation. It is also useful when the coat is shedding, although this is minimal in Greyhounds.

- Fine-toothed comb – to work through the coat, also helps to remove dead hair when a Greyhound is shedding.

- Chamois leather – to bring out the shine in the coat.

- Nail-clippers – the guillotine type are easy to use.

- Toothbrush and toothpaste – choose between a long-handled toothbrush or a finger brush, whichever you find easiest to use. There are flavoured canine toothpastes on the market which are acceptable to your dog.

Toys

A racing Greyhound is not brought up to play and as this behaviour has not been reinforced, it can fade to the point of being almost non-existent. However there are exceptions to the rule, and some Greyhound can be motivated by toys and will enjoy games of tug or retrieve.

But even if your Greyhound does not want to play, you should invest in a rubber kong.

This is a hard rubber toy, which comes in different sizes, and can be stuffed with food.

This provides an ideal source of occupation for your Greyhound at times when you cannot be with him.

Finding a vet

Before your Greyhound arrives home, you should register with a vet. Visit several vets in your local area, or speak to other pet owners that you might know, to see who they recommend. It is so important to find a good vet – almost as much as finding a good doctor for yourself. You need to find someone with whom you can build up a good rapport and have complete faith in. Word of mouth is really the best recommendation. When you contact a veterinary practice, find out the following:

- Does the surgery run an appointment system?

- What are the arrangements for emergency, out of hours cover?

- What facilities are available at the practice?

- Do any of the vets in the practice have experience treating Greyhounds?

This is particular important as Greyhounds have a very low tolerance to anaesthesia. You therefore need a vet who fully understands this issue in case your dog ever requires surgery. If you are satisfied with what your find, and the staff appear to be helpful and friendly, book an appointment so your Greyhound can have a health check a couple of days after you collect him.

Facing page: You need to find a vet who understands Greyhounds as a breed.

Settling in

When you first arrive home with your Greyhound, be careful not to overwhelm him. You and your family are hugely excited, but your Greyhound is in a completely strange environment with new sounds, smells and sights...

Some Greyhounds may have been cared for in a foster home prior to adoption, but the vast majority will have spent their entire lives in kennels and will be entering a house for the very first time.

This is a daunting experience, even for the boldest of dogs, so you need to watch your Greyhound's body language which will give you clues as to how he is feeling. Do not attempt to rush him; monitor his reactions and progress at a pace he is comfortable with.

First, let him explore the garden. He will probably need to relieve himself after the journey home, so take him to the allocated toileting area and, when he performs, give him plenty of praise. Give him

a chance to sniff and to get his bearings. If you take things gradually, you will see him grow in confidence. Wait until he is beginning to show more relaxed behaviour before you introduce him to the house.

When you take your Greyhound indoors, your first port of call should be the kitchen or wherever you have located his sleeping quarters. Allow him to investigate and then show him his crate – maybe encouraging him to go in by throwing a treat through the open door.

Let him have a sniff, and allow him to go in and out as he wants to. Later on, when he is tired, you can put him in the crate while you stay in the same room. In this way he will learn to settle and will not think he is being abandoned. Some owners place a blanket over the crate, covering the back and sides, so that it is even more cosy and den-like.

Meeting the family

Resist the temptation of inviting friends and neighbours to come and meet the new arrival; your Greyhound needs to focus on getting to know his new family for the first few days. Try not to swamp him with too much attention; let him make the decision and come to you. If he is not pressurised, he will relax much more quickly.

If you have children in the family, you need to keep everything as calm as possible. Hopefully, your Greyhound was able to meet all members of his family at the rehoming centre, but he will not be familiar with children and will find them strange and unpredictable.

A Greyhound can be easily alarmed by too much noise, by small children rushing around, or being approached suddenly and without warning. The best plan is to get the children to sit on the floor and give them all a treat. Each child can then call him, stroke him, and offer a treat. In this way the Greyhound is making the decisions rather than being forced into interactions he may find stressful.

Involve all family members with the day-to-day care of your Greyhound; this will enable the bond to develop with the whole family as opposed to just one person. Encourage the children to train and reward him, teaching him to respond to them and respect them. In return you must teach your children to treat your Greyhound with respect. He must not be prodded or poked like a plaything, he must never be disturbed when his eating, or when he goes to his bed or to his crate. If these rules are observed, relationships will blossom and your Greyhound will soon be an integral member of the family.

The animal family

Care must be taken when introducing your Greyhound to a resident dog to ensure that relations get off on the right footing. Ex-racers are used to living with their own kind, and so there will rarely be a problem if you are adding another Greyhound to your tribe. That said, you should never take anything for granted, and introductions should be conducted with tact and diplomacy.

If you have a small dog, you will have already ensured that the Greyhound of your choice does not have a chase issue in relation to small dogs but, again, you cannot be too careful. The best policy is to proceed at a steady pace so you can monitor what is going on.

If you are lucky, you will have been allowed to take your resident dog to the rehoming centre so initial meeting and greeting is on neutral territory. But if this has not been possible, allow your dog to smell the Greyhound's bedding (and vice versa if feasible) before they actually meet so they are familiar with each other's scent.

The garden is the best place for introductions as your resident dog will not feel so protective about his home territory. Recruit a family member so you can keep both dogs on-lead. It is important to keep the leads loose so the dogs do not feel they are getting outside support; they need to move freely so they can sniff each other. Try not to interfere as this is the natural way that dogs get to know each other.

You will only need to intervene if either dog is too boisterous and alarms the other. If this happens, slow down the proceedings. Open up a space between the two dogs and maybe walk around the garden, gradually getting closer, before allowing a close-up interaction.

If you are sensitive to both dogs, it rarely takes long for the pair to accept each other.

Below: Initial interactions between dogs should always be supervised.

Obviously, they will need more time to establish an on-going relationship but if the initial meeting goes well, and you continue to give active supervision over the next couple of weeks, the dogs will learn to live in harmony.

But no matter how well the two dogs seem to be getting on during this settling in period, do not leave them alone unless one is crated.

Feline friends

The Greyhound is a sighthound, bred to hunt and chase, and a cat will, in most instances, trigger his prey instinct.

However, as already highlighted (See What can you expect from your Greyhound?), there are some Greyhounds with a low prey drive, labelled as non-chasers, who can be trusted with the family cat.

There are also Greyhounds that have been successful on the track and can be re-educated to live with a cat.

The rehoming charity will conduct tests to see if a Greyhound is cat friendly and this will, obviously, influence your choice of Greyhound. However, when you are introducing a cat and a Greyhound, you must proceed with the utmost caution. It may be easier if the cat is confined in a carrier for the first couple of meetings so your Greyhound has a chance to make his acquaintance in a controlled situation.

Keep talking to your Greyhound and rewarding him for giving you attention so that he does not focus too intently on the cat. If your Greyhound is remaining calm, progress to allowing the cat to roam free, but make sure your dog is muzzled and hold him on a loose lead so you remain in control.

Again, talk to your Greyhound and reward him with a treat every time he looks away from the cat. The next stage is to allow your Greyhound off-lead, but make sure the cat has an easy escape route, just in case he tries to chase.

This is an on-going process but all the time your Greyhound is learning that he is rewarded for ignoring the cat. In time, the novelty will wear off and the pair will mostly ignore each other. In some cases, a Greyhound and the family cat will become the best of friends and end up sharing a bed!

Feeding

The rehoming charity will give you information about the diet they have been feeding, and it is best to stick with this for the first few weeks. A change in diet is likely to cause digestive upset and you do not want your Greyhound to be struggling with this, along with

There are instances of real friendship between a Greyhound and the family cat.

all the stress of moving home. Some Greyhounds are real foodies, others are not so keen, but it may take a couple of days before your Greyhound feels relaxed enough to eat up his food. If he seems disinterested in his food, give him 10 minutes to eat what he wants and then remove the leftovers and start afresh at the next meal. Obviously if you have any concerns about your Greyhound in the first few days, seek advice from your vet.

It is important to give your dog space where he can eat in peace. If you have children, you need to establish a rule that no one is to go near the dog when he is feeding.

Greyhounds are not known for guarding food, but you can prevent this from happening by giving your dog half his ration, and then dropping food around his bowl. This will stop him guarding his bowl and, at the same time, he will see your presence in a positive light. You can also call him away from the bowl and reward him with food – maybe something extra special – which he can take from your hand.

Start doing this as soon as your Greyhound arrives in his new home, and continue working on it throughout his life.

Facing page: Be patient as your Greyhound adapts to his new life.

The first night

An ex-racing Greyhound is used to being kennelled and so, theoretically, your dog should not feel anxious when he is left alone at night. However, the environment is very different, and he may feel disorientated.

The best plan is to establish a nighttime routine, and then stick to it so that your Greyhound knows what is expected of him.

Take him out into the garden to relieve himself, and then settle him in his crate. Some owners leave a low light on, others have tried a radio as company. Like people, Greyhounds are all individuals and what works for one, does not necessarily work for another, so it is a matter of trial and error.

Be very positive when you leave your Greyhound on his own; do not linger or keep returning as this will make the situation more stressful.

He may protest to begin with, but if you stick to your routine, he will accept that he gets left at night but you always return in the morning.

Facing page: Establish a night-time routine so your Greyhound learns to settle.

House training

Greyhounds are naturally clean animals and although your dog may have lived all his life in kennels, it will not take him long to learn to be clean in the house.

The key to successful house training is vigilance and consistency. If you establish a routine, and you stick to it, your Greyhound will understand what is required.

As discussed earlier, it is a good idea to allocate a toileting area in the garden so your Greyhound builds up an association and knows why you are taking him outside.

Establish a routine and make sure you take your Greyhound out at the following times:

- First thing in the morning

- After mealtimes

- On waking from a sleep
- Last thing at night.

A puppy needs to be taken out to relieve himself every two hours as an absolute minimum. This is not necessary for an adult dog but try to keep to a schedule so your Greyhound adjusts to a new regime. Start using a verbal cue, such as 'Busy', when he is performing and, in time, this will trigger the desired response.

Do not be tempted to put your Greyhound out on the doorstep in the hope that he will toilet on his own. The likelihood is that he will simply sit there, waiting to get back inside the house!

No matter how bad the weather, accompany your Greyhound and give him lots of praise when he performs correctly. You can reward him with a food treat, but it is best to do this on a random basis so he does not always expect it.

When accidents happen

In most cases, an adult Greyhound will make the transition from kennel dog to house dog in no time at all. If he does have the occasional lapse, try not to make a big thing of it, particularly as it will probably have happened in your absence.

Your Greyhound will not connect an action, which may have happened some time ago, with the consequence of being reprimanded.

Do not be fooled by his 'guilty' look; he is simply reacting to the telling off – he has absolutely no idea why he is in trouble.

If you discover a mess in the house, clear it up with the minimum of fuss and try to work out why it happened.

Did you leave it too long between trips to the garden?

Did your Greyhound get hot after a walk and drink more water than usual?

Could it be that he was worried about being left home alone?

If you work at establishing a house training regime over the first few weeks, it is highly unlikely that you will have longterm problems.

Stick to the time honoured rules of house training: be calm, be consistent and be vigilant.

Choosing
a diet

A racing Greyhound needs to run at maximum speed for short bursts, which puts huge demands on the body. The skill of a trainer is feeding a top-quality diet that enables peak performance. However, your newly adopted Greyhound is now leading a very different life and his diet should reflect this.

When a Greyhound is racing once or twice a week, he needs a high-quality diet, with protein making up 24-27 per cent of the total intake. The rest of the meal is made up of vitamins and minerals, carbohydrates, fats and fatty acids.

Trainers all have their own methods of feeing, but the most commonly fed diet is made up of a complete food, meat, gravy and vegetables.

When a Greyhound retires, the amount of energy he expends will drop dramatically. Instead of speeding round the track and being schooled on gallops, he will be getting gentle on-lead exercise, with occasional opportunities to free run.

When choosing a diet for an ex-racer, the general principle is that the protein level should drop to 20 per cent. There are basically three categories of diet to choose from:

Complete

This is probably the most popular diet as it is easy to feed and is specially formulated with all the nutrients your dog needs. This means that you should not add any supplements or you may upset the nutritional balance.

Most complete diets come in different life stages: puppy, adult maintenance and senior, so this means that your Greyhound is getting what he needs during adulthood and as he becomes older. You can even get prescription diets for dogs with particular health issues.

There are many different brands to choose from so it is advisable to seek advice from the rehoming charity which will have lengthy experience of feeding ex-racing Greyhounds.

Canned/pouches

This type of food is usually fed with hard biscuit, and most Greyhounds find it very appetising. However, the ingredients and the nutritional value do vary significantly between the different brands so you will need to check the label.

This type of food often has a high moisture content, so you need to be sure your Greyhound is getting all the nutrition he needs.

Homemade

There are some owners who like to prepare meals especially for their dogs – and it is probably much appreciated. The danger is that although the food is tasty, and your Greyhound may enjoy the variety, you cannot be sure that it has the correct nutritional balance.

If this is a route you want to go down, you will need to find out the exact ratio of fats, carbohydrates, proteins, minerals and vitamins that are needed, which is quite an undertaking.

The Barf (Biologically Appropriate Raw Food) diet is another, more natural approach to feeding. Dogs are fed a diet mimicking what they would have eaten in the wild, consisting of raw meat, bone, muscle, fat, and vegetable matter.

Greyhounds do well on this diet so it is certainly worthy of consideration. There are now a number of companies that specialise in producing the Barf diet in frozen form, which will make your job a lot easier.

Feeding regime

In many racing kennels, the day starts with a light cereal breakfast, and the main meal is fed early afternoon, obviously dependent on whether the dog is racing on that day. You may wish to mimic this, or you may prefer to split the rations between two meals: morning and evening. This is entirely a matter for your convenience.

Regardless of the regime you choose, you must not exercise your Greyhound before of after he has eaten. It is best to leave a minimum of one hour either side of mealtimes otherwise you run the risk of your Greyhound going down with bloat. As previously mentioned, a raised feeding bowl aids digestion and minimises the risk of both bloat and constipation.

Keep a close eye on your Greyhound's condition to see if he is thriving on the diet you are providing.

You may decide to keep to the diet recommended by the rehoming charity, and if your Greyhound is thriving there is no need to change. However, if he is not doing well on the food, or you have problems with supply, you will need to make a change.

When switching diets, it is very important to do it on a gradual basis, changing over from one food to the next, a little at a time, and spreading the transition over a week to 10 days. This will avoid the risk of digestive upset.

Bones and chews

Bones and chews are an excellent way of promoting dental health; gnawing a bone helps to remove tartar from teeth, it freshens and it will also give your Greyhound hours of entertainment.

Raw marrow bones are the best and safest bone to offer but, even so, they should only be given under supervision.

White, sterilised bones do not make so much mess as a raw marrow bone, and they have the same end result of helping to keep your dog's teeth clean.

Rawhide chews are best avoided; it is all too easy for a Greyhound to bite off a chunk and swallow it, with the danger of it then causing a blockage.

Facing page: The amount you feed needs to be matched with your Greyhound's energy output.

Weighed in

Greyhounds seem to be divided into two camps: those that eat well and put on weight, and those that are not particularly keen on their food and struggle to maintain a healthy weight. You will need to find out what is 'normal' for your dog in terms of his ideal weight. The rehoming charity will keep a record of each dog's weight during their time in kennels and this will give you a good starting point.

As your Greyhound adapts to life as a domestic pet, his weight may change a little, but you certainly do not want to see any drastic changes in terms of either weight increase or decrease. Most racing Greyhounds are fed meat and gravy along with their complete diet, and if your Greyhound is failing to eat a complete diet without supplements, this could well be the reason.

You do not want to pamper your Greyhound, otherwise you run the risk of turning him into a faddy feeder. Equally, you do not want to upset the nutritional balance of his diet. The best way of getting round this is by adding a little gravy which will make the food more appetising without adding extras. You need to bear in mind that refusing food is also a sign of ill health. If your dog refuses food for more than 24 hours you need to observe his behaviour to see if there are any attendant problems and seek advice from your vet. It could be that you have the opposite problem and you are worried that your Greyhound is putting on too much weight. Despite their naturally athletic build, a Greyhound can become obese, and this has serious health implications.

An overweight dog can suffer from heart disease, diabetes, malfunction of the liver, increased blood pressure, as well as putting excessive strain on the joints and ligaments. It is a fact that obese dogs have a shortened life expectancy.

When looking at your Greyhound, you want to see an athletic outline; an outer rib or two may be visible, but you do not want to see the entire ribcage. Looking along his back, you should see a smooth line; you do not want to see the vertebrae or the hip bones standing out. Viewed from above, your Greyhound should have a definite waist where his loins are located. If you are concerned about your Greyhound's weight – whether he is overweight or underweight – get into the habit of giving him regular weigh-ins at your veterinary practice so you can keep an accurate check on him. If he is putting on too much weight or losing weight, ask for a consultation with your vet who can help you plan a suitable diet.

Caring for your Greyhound

The Greyhound is a low maintenance breed in terms of coat care and his exercise requirements are moderate but, like all animals, he has his own special needs which you must take on board.

Getting started

All racing Greyhounds are groomed and massaged as part of their care and fitness regime, so you will have a head start in that your dog will be accustomed to being handled. This is a great bonus as handling a large dog that is unfamiliar with invasive treatment could be highly problematical.

Make sure your dog is standing on a non-slippery surface when you groom him or carry out routine care. This may involve putting down a rubber mat to give him a firm footing. If your Greyhound feels insecure, his anxiety will increase and he will create

a bad association with all forms of handling.

It is very rare for a Greyhound to be intolerant to handling and grooming. However, if your dog is sensitive, take your time so you do not increase his anxiety. Have some tasty treats to hand and reward him after you have given him a few strokes with the brush, around the shoulder area.

He will be able to see what you are doing, and you are not being invasive. If he is concerned, repeat what you have done a few times and then end your grooming session. Do not move on to more sensitive areas until he accepts what you are doing. Proceed step by step, giving lots of rewards, and he will soon learn to accept your attentions. You may think this is a lot of trouble to go to with a short-coated breed that needs minimal grooming. But there are times when your Greyhound will need to be examined by a vet, and this will be so much easier if he is relaxed.

A grooming session also provides an excellent opportunity to give your dog a thorough check over. If you see any signs of trouble – a bald, area, a sore spot, or an unusual lump or bump – you will be able to treat it before it gets worse or, if necessary, refer it to your vet.

Coat care

When you are grooming your Greyhound, it helps if you stick to a routine. This ensures you do a thorough job and your Greyhound will know what to expect: Start by working through the coat with a fine-toothed comb. The coat lies close to the skin, and there is very little body fat. You therefore need to be firm but gentle as you comb so you do not cause any discomfort. When you work through the coat in this way, you get a close-up view so you can detect any signs of parasites, such a fleas, or more particularly flea dirts, which you can treat accordingly. For more information, see Health Care.

Now use a stiff-bristled body brush; some owners opt for a horse dandy brush which works well on the Greyhound's sleek coat. You can be a little more vigorous in your grooming, using strong, firm brush strokes which will remove dirt and debris from the coat. A rubber mitt or hound glove is useful to massage your Greyhound and helps to remove dead hairs. As a Greyhound does not have an undercoat, shedding is not as extensive as in other breeds, but it is significant at certain times of the year. If you want your Greyhound to look his best, you can finish by giving him an all over polish with a chamois leather which brings out the shine in his coat.

Bathing

Bathing should be kept to a minimum as it has an adverse effect on the skin's natural oils. Not only does this result in a dull coat, it can also cause a dry, itchy skin. We are fortunate that the Greyhound does not often go in for rolling in foul-smelling substances – but there are always exceptions to the rule. The lack of undercoat reduces dog odour, but there are times when your Greyhound may be in need of a freshen up.

You will probably use your bath or show cubicle, so use a rubber matt to give your Greyhound a firm footing. If you are using a bath, a shower appliance attached to the taps, will make your job a lot easier. Use a mild moisturising shampoo, specially formulated for dogs and work it into a rich lather. Rinse thoroughly and then apply a conditioner which will improve the quality and appearance of the coat. Rinse the coat to ensure there are no remaining traces of shampoo or conditioner and then towel dry while your Greyhound is still in the bath/shower. If it is cold, settle him on some cosy bedding If the weather is warm, he can dry off in the garden. If it is a bright day, you may be able to find him a sunspot where he can stretch out and relax – a Greyhound's idea of heaven!

Facing page: The Greyhound's coat needs minimal care.

Routine care

In addition to grooming, you will need to carry out some routine care.

Eyes

Check the eyes for signs of soreness or discharge. You can use a piece of cotton wool (cotton) – a separate piece for each eye – and wipe away any debris.

Ears

The ears should be clean and free from odour. You can buy specially manufactured ear wipes, or you can use a piece of cotton wool to clean them if necessary. Do not probe into the ear canal or you risk doing more harm than good.

Teeth

Dental disease is becoming more prevalent among dogs so teeth cleaning should be seen as an essential part of your care regime.

The build up of tartar on the teeth can result in tooth decay, gum infection and bad breath, and if it is allowed to accumulate, you may have no option but to get the teeth cleaned under anaesthetic.

Again, your Greyhound will be used to his teeth

*Routine care prevents
health problems arising.*

being cleaned during his days as a racing dog, so he should accept the procedure. However, it is a good idea to reward your Greyhound when he co-operates and then he will positively look forward to his teeth-cleaning sessions.

Nails

Nail trimming is a task dreaded by many owners, but your Greyhound will be used to the routine and should not fight against it.

Nails may be white or black depending on coat colour. If the nail is white, you will be able to see the quick (the vein that runs through the nail), but it is obscured in dark-coloured nails. If you cut the quick it will bleed profusely and cause considerable discomfort.

The best policy is to trim little and often so the nails don't grow too long, and you do not risk cutting too much and catching the quick.

If you are worried about trimming your Greyhound's nails, go to your vet so you can see it done properly.

If you are still concerned, you can always use the services of a professional groomer.

Exercise

As already highlighted, a Greyhound does not requires extensive exercise, but he requires sufficient to keep his muscles toned and to maintain his general fitness. Exercise provides mental stimulation as your dog can explore new places, and you will both enjoy the quality time you spend together.

Because of a Greyhound's strong prey instinct, most exercise will be conducted on lead. This may not use up as much energy as free running but it will keep your Greyhound fit, and if you change your route, he will be interested and alert as he takes in different sights and sounds.

You can walk along roads, go to parks, and also explore the countryside. If you want to extend your Greyhound's freedom so he can go further ahead and has the opportunity to sniff, you can use a longer lead, or a long line, providing you have good control.

Extending leads can be used, but as already stated, they are not ideal for Greyhounds. There is no better sight than seeing a Greyhound at full stretch, and you be able to do this if you choose your exercise area with care. A beach is ideal, as you will never lose sight of your dog.

Foraging for fun

A Greyhound needs mental stimulation as well as physical exercise and a good way of providing this is to do a food scatter, using kibble from a complete diet.

Instead of giving your dog his meal in a bowl, take him out to the garden, and scatter the food over a small area. Your Greyhound will have to sniff out his food, which makes him use his brain – and he gets instant rewards for his foraging behaviour.

When he gets used to the idea, you can scatter the food over a wider area so he has to work harder to find it all. Mental exertion is as tiring as physical exercise so a food scatter is ideal if you are short of time and cannot give your Greyhound his full quota of exercise.

If you choose an unpopular time, such as early in the morning, you are unlikely to encounter other dog walkers. You may have access to an enclosed field, which will give your Greyhound a chance to run. Obviously, you need to ensure he has a good recall before you try this. Swimming is a useful form of exercise, particularly for a Greyhound who has sustained an injury during his racing career as it allows him to use his body without putting pressure on the joints.

Some Greyhounds enjoy swimming, others can't bear to get their feet wet, so you will have to find out whether your dog is happy in the water. If you take your Greyhound swimming, you need to be aware of potential dangers. Check that the water is calm, with no currents or undertow if your dog is swimming in the sea. You also need to make sure that there is easy access back to dry land. When your Greyhound has finished his swimming session, towel him dry and put on a warm fleece coat, unless the weather is hot.

The older Greyhound

We are fortunate that the Greyhound has a pretty good life expectancy – generally around 12 years, and some may do slightly better. As your Greyhound grows older, he may sleep more and he may be reluctant to go for longer walks. He may show signs of stiffness when he gets up from his bed, but these generally ease when he starts moving.

Some older Greyhounds may have impaired vision, and some may become a little deaf, but as long as their senses do not deteriorate dramatically, this is something older dogs learn to live with.

If you treat your older dog with kindness and consideration, he will enjoy his later years and suffer the minimum of discomfort. It is advisable to switch him over to a senior diet, which is more suited to his needs. The older Greyhound will often prefer a softer diet, and you will need to keep a close check on his teeth as these may cause problems.

Make sure his sleeping quarters are warm and free from draughts, and if he gets wet, make sure you dry him thoroughly. Most important of all, be guided by your Greyhound. He will have good days when he feels up to going for a walk, and other days when he would prefer to potter in the garden.

If you have a younger dog at home, this may well stimulate your Greyhound to take more of an interest in what is going on, but make sure he is not pestered as he needs to rest undisturbed when he is tired.

Letting go

Inevitably there comes a time when your Greyhound is not enjoying a good quality of life, and you need to make the painful decision to let him go. We would all wish that our dogs died, painlessly, in their sleep but, unfortunately, this is rarely the case.

However, we can allow our dogs to die with dignity, and to suffer as little as possible, and this should be our way of saying thank you for the wonderful companionship they have given us.

When you feel the time is drawing close, talk to your vet who will be able to make an objective assessment of your Greyhound's condition and will help you to make the right decision.

This is the hardest thing you will ever have to do as a dog owner, and it is only natural to grieve for your beloved Greyhound. But eventually you will be able to look back on the happy memories of times spent together, and this will bring much comfort.

You may, in time, feel that your life is not complete without a Greyhound and you will feel ready to adopt again. There are many Greyhounds in need of homes so it would be a fitting tribute to provide a forever home for another of these magnificent creatures.

You will have many happy memories of your beloved Greyhound.

Social skills

When you take on a puppy you need to plan a programme of socialisation so that he learns to cope with life as a companion dog. It is just the same for an ex-racing Greyhound who has very limited experience of the outside world.

Early learning

Your Greyhound will not be used to living in a home, and there may be some aspects that he finds alarming. When he first arrives, allow him to investigate the house – but bear in mind there may be unexpected shocks in store for him, such as the noise of the vacuum cleaner or the washing machine, and those unexpected noises from the radio and television.

Do not take anything for granted; allocate time to introduce your Greyhound to all these new experiences, and he will soon learn to accept them.

To begin with, your Greyhound needs to get used to all the members of his new family, but then you should give him the opportunity to meet friends and other people who visit your home.

This will be a totally novel experience, and your

Greyhound needs to learn that if you are happy to welcome someone into your home, he has nothing to worry about.

If your dog seems concerned, keep him on lead, and feed him treats as you allow the visitor into your house. When your Greyhound is relaxed, ask the visitor to feed him a couple of treats. The Greyhound is not a guarding breed, and it will not take long for him to accept all newcomers.

If you do not have children, make arrangements so your Greyhound has the chance to meet and play with other people's children, ensuring that interactions are always supervised.

The outside world

Your Greyhound will have very limited experience of the world beyond the racing track and kennels, so you need to start a socialisation programme which will introduce him to a wide variety of different situations. In most cases, your Greyhound will have good lead-walking manners which will make your task easier.

Start socialising your Greyhound in a quiet area with light traffic, and only progress to a busier place when he is ready. There is so much to see and hear – people (maybe carrying bags or umbrellas), pushchairs, bicycles, cars, lorries, machinery – so give your dog a chance to take it all in.

If he does appear worried, do not fall into the trap of sympathising with him or over-doing the reassurance. This will only teach your Greyhound that he had a good reason to be worried.

Instead, give him a little space so he does not have to confront whatever he is frightened of, and distract him with a few treats. Then encourage him to walk past, using an encouraging tone of voice, never forcing him by yanking on the lead. Reward him for any forward movement and your Greyhound will soon learn that he can trust you, and there is nothing to fear.

Meeting and greeting

Your Greyhound will be used to living with his own kind, but he will be unfamiliar with other dogs. In the rehoming centre, he will have been tested to see if is able to live with small dogs – which can trigger his chase instinct – but he will have no experience of getting to know other dogs, which come in many different guises. The best plan is to meet up with dog-owning friends so you can start to broaden your Greyhound's friendship circle. Make sure the dogs in question are of sound temperament so your Greyhound only has good experiences.

Facing page: If your Greyhound can be trusted off-lead, seek out opportunities where he can run and play.

Adopt the following procedures:

Try to find a meeting place that is on neutral territory so neither dogs feels his space is being threatened. Ideally this would be a safe place where you can, eventually, allow the dogs off-lead. To begin with, keep both dogs on lead and allow the dogs to walk alongside each other some distance apart. Talk to your Greyhound and when he focuses on you, reward him with a treat. Gradually narrow the gap, again rewarding your Greyhound when he give you attention.

If both dogs are calm and relaxed, allow the two dogs to meet, keeping them on loose leads so they can sniff each other. Remind your dog you are still on the end of the lead, by calling him and then rewarding him when he looks at you. If all is well, allow the dogs off-lead so they are free to develop their relationship.

Training classes

A training class will give your Greyhound the opportunity to work alongside other dogs in a controlled situation, and he will also learn to focus on you in a different, distracting environment. However, the training class needs to be of the highest calibre or you risk doing more harm than good. Before you go along with your Greyhound, attend a class as an observer to make sure you are happy with what goes on.

Find out the following:

- How much training experience do the instructors have?

- Are the classes divided into appropriate age categories?

- Do the instructors have experience training Greyhounds?

- Do they use positive, reward-based training methods?

If the training class is well run, it is certainly worth attending. Both you and your Greyhound will learn useful training exercises; it will increase his social skills, and you will have the chance to talk to lots of like-minded dog enthusiasts.

Below: Give your Greyhound the opportunity to meet other breeds.

Training guidelines

The Greyhound is a good-natured dog who will soon learn to adapt to family life. However, he has missed out on some steps in his education which you will need to remedy.

You will be keen to get started but in your rush to get training underway, do not neglect the fundamentals which could make the difference between success and failure.

You need to get into the mindset of a Greyhound working out what motivates him and, equally, what makes him switch off. Decide on your priorities for training, and then think of ways of making your training as much fun – and as positive – as possible.

When you start training, try to observe the following guidelines:

Choose an area that is free from distractions so your Greyhound will focus on you. You can move on to a more challenging environment as learning progresses.

Do not train your Greyhound just after he has eaten or when you have returned from exercise. He will either be too full, or too tired, to concentrate.

Do not train if you are in a bad mood, or if you are short of time. These sessions always end in disaster!

Providing a worthwhile reward is an essential tool in training. In most cases, a Greyhound will make the effort if he is working for food.

Make sure food rewards are high value, e.g. cooked liver, cheese or sausage, so your Greyhound has a real incentive.

Keep your verbal cues simple, and always use the same one for each exercise. For example, when you ask your Greyhound to go into the down position, the cue is "down", not "lie down, "get down", or anything else. Remember, your Greyhound does not speak English; he associates the sound of the word with the action.

If your dog is finding an exercise difficult, break it down into small steps so it is easier to understand.

Do not make your training sessions boring and repetitious; your Greyhound will lose concentration and will cease to co-operate.

Training should always be a rewarding experience for your Greyhound

Do not train for too long, and always end training sessions on a good note. If your Greyhound is tired and making mistakes, ask him to do a simple exercise so you have the opportunity to praise and reward him. You may well find that he benefits from having a break and will make better progress next time you try.

Above all, make training fun so you and your Greyhound enjoy spending quality time together.

First lessons

As your Greyhound settles in his new home, you will discover what he knows, and what he needs to learn. As already highlighted, you will be focusing on a programme of socialisation, but you will also need to teach some basic obedience exercises.

Walking on the lead

Racing Greyhounds are exercised on lead so your Greyhound should have mastered this exercise. However, the Greyhound is a big dog, with considerable strength, and some dogs may have got into the habit of pulling on the lead.

It is essential to rectify this as lead walking will be your Greyhound's principal form of exercise.

Try the following:

Restrict lead training to the garden in the initial stages so you are working in an environment that is free from distractions. Walk a few paces, being very aware of any tension on the lead. If you feel the lead tighten and your Greyhound is attempting to get ahead of you, stop, change direction, and set off again.

Your Greyhound needs to understand that pulling ahead has exactly the opposite effect to the one he wants. Rather than calling the tune, he has to co-operate with you. Keep a good supply of tasty treats and remember only reward – with food and with verbal praise – when he is walking by your side on a loose lead.

The mistake made by many owners at this stage is to use the treats to lure the dog into position rather than rewarding him for the correct behaviour.

Keep training sessions short, and when you are ready, venture into the outside world.

Do not be too ambitious to begin with. Build up the level of distraction and the duration of lead walking only when your Greyhound is consistently showing the behaviour you want.

Let your Greyhound dictate the pace of training.

Stationary exercises

For most dogs, teaching a sit and a down are the key ingredients of basic obedience, but you will need to adapt this. A Greyhound's conformation means that sitting on his hindquarters is uncomfortable, so there is little point in teaching him this exercise.

The only practical application is if your want your Greyhound to sit briefly before you give him his food. This is useful if your Greyhound is a bit of a foodie and may try to get to his bowl before you put it down.

When you have prepared your Greyhound's meal, hold the bowl above his nose. As he looks up, he will naturally lower his hindquarters and sit. Reward him by placing his food bowl on the floor. Repeat this a few times, and when your Greyhound understands what is required, introduce the verbal cue, "sit".

Down

Your Greyhound will not stay in position when he is sitting, so it is all the more important to teach a reliable down. This exercise can be used in many different situations and an instant response can be a lifesaver.

Once your Greyhound responds to the verbal cue "down", you can work on duration.

For most dogs you would start this exercise from a sit but with a Greyhound, it is easier if you train him from a stand.

Stand in front of your dog and show him you have a treat in your hand. Hold the treat just in front of his nose and slowly lower it towards the ground, between his front legs.

As your Greyhound follows the treat he will go down on his front legs and, in a few moments, his hindquarters will follow. Close your hand over the treat so he doesn't cheat and get the treat before he is in the correct position. As soon as he is in the down, give him the treat and lots of praise.

Keep practising, and when your Greyhound understands what you want, introduce the verbal cue, "down".

Come when called

There will be limited opportunities for free running your Greyhound but this does not mean that your should neglect the recall. If you are confident that your Greyhound will return, you will be more likely to seek out free running opportunities for him.

Your aim must be to make coming when called even more rewarding than sniffing or exploring. This needs to be built up over a period of time, with lots of repetition so your Greyhound is 100 per cent confident that he will always be rewarded.

Start your recall training at home when your Greyhound is in a confined space, such as the kitchen. This is a good place to build up a positive association with the verbal cue – particularly if you ask him to "come" to get his dinner!

The next stage is to transfer the lesson to the garden. Arm yourself with some high value treats, and wait until your Greyhound is distracted. Then call him, using a higher-pitched, excited tone of voice. Give lots of verbal encouragement and reward him as soon as he reaches you. Keep practising so you build up a really positive association with the verbal cue, "come".

Now you are ready to introduce some distractions. Try calling your Greyhound when someone else is in the garden, or wait a few minutes until he is investigating a really interesting scent. When he responds, make a really big fuss of him and give him extra treats so he knows it is worth his while to come to you.

If he is slow to come, run away a few steps and then call again, making yourself sound really exciting. Jump up and down, open your arms wide to welcome him; it doesn't matter how silly you look, he needs to see you as the most fun person in the world.

When you have a reliable recall in the garden, you can venture into the outside world. Obviously, you will need to pick your exercise area with care. Initially, try a recall with the minimum of distractions so you can be more certain of success.

Do not make the mistake of only asking your

Greyhound to come at the end of his allotted exercise period. What is the incentive in coming back to you if all you do is clip on his lead, marking the end of his free time? Instead, call your dog at random times, giving him a treat and a stroke, and then letting him go free again. In this way, coming to you – and focusing on you – is always rewarding.

Be ready with a reward when your Greyhound comes back to you.

Control exercises

These exercises are not the most exciting, but they make day to day living so much easier.

Wait

This exercise teaches your Greyhound to wait in position until you give the next command; it differs from the stay exercise where he must stay where you have left him for a more prolonged period. The most useful application of the wait exercise is when you are getting your dog out of the car and you need him to stay in position until you clip on his lead.

Start with your Greyhound on the lead to give you a greater chance of success. You can teach this exercise from the stand or the down. Once he is in position, stand in front of him.

Step back one pace, holding your hand, palm flat, facing him. Wait a second and then come back to stand in front of him. You can then reward him and

release him with a word, such as "OK".

Practise this a few times, waiting a little longer before you reward him, and then introduce the verbal cue, "wait". You can reinforce the lesson by using it in different situations, such as asking your Greyhound to "wait" before you put his food bowl down or when you have opened the front door and you want him to follow you out.

Stay

Start with your Greyhound in the down as he is most likely to be secure in this position. Stand by his side and then step forwards, using a hand signal (palm towards your dog) to 'block' his advance.

Step back, release him, and then reward him. Practise until your Greyhound understands the exercise and then introduce the verbal cue, "stay". Gradually increase the distance you can leave your Greyhound, and increase the challenge by walking around him so that he learns he must stay until you release him.

When he is staying in position at a distance, you can work on duration, increasing the length of time he stays in the down.

Off

The Greyhound is an easy-going animal and he is unlikely to show guarding behaviour. However, he is keen on his comforts and he can be hard to move once he has got himself settled. Obviously, this is not a problem if he is on his bed or in his crate, but if he is allowed on the sofa – and he is taking up all the room – you need to shift him without conflict.

When you are teaching this exercise, make it easy for your Greyhound by putting some bedding on the floor and then asking him to move. The bedding is not high value, and if your ask your Greyhound to move after a few moments, he will not be fully settled. Make sure you have some tasty treats, and when your Greyhound is lying on the bedding, show him a treat in your hand and stand a few paces away so he has to get up.

As soon as he responds, reward him with the treat and with lots of verbal praise. Keep practising, but on different occasions so you are not constantly nagging your Greyhound when he tries to settle. When he understands what you want, introduce the verbal cue, "off". You can now try the exercise in different locations, such as when your Greyhound is on the sofa. Now that he knows he will get a treat if he moves, he will be ready to co-operate.

Opportunities for Greyhounds

The Greyhound's true talent lies in running at speed and so working closely with his human owner does not come naturally. However, the Greyhound is remarkably adaptable and if you use positive, reward-based training methods, he will expand his skill base.

Good Citizen Scheme

The Kennel Club Good Citizen Scheme was introduced to promote responsible dog ownership, and to teach dogs basic good manners. In the US there is one test; in the UK there are four award levels: Puppy Foundation, Bronze, Silver and Gold.

Exercises within the scheme include:

- Walking on lead

- Road walking

- Control at door/gate.

- Food manners

- Recall

- Stay

- Send to bed

- Emergency stop.

- Rally O

A Greyhound is unlikely to enjoy competitive obedience as the discipline demands a high degree of accuracy and precision which does not suit his temperament, nor his physique. However, there is no reason not to try Rally O.

This is loosely based on Obedience, and also has a

few exercises borrowed from Agility when you get to the highest levels. Handler and dog must complete a course, in the designated order, which has a variety of different exercises which could number from 12 to 20.

The course is timed and the team must complete within the time limit that is set, but there are no bonus marks for speed.

The great advantage of Rally O is that it is very relaxed, and anyone can compete; indeed, it has proved very popular for handlers with disabilities as they are able to work their dogs to a high standard and compete on equal terms with other competitors.

Agility

This is a challenging sport, which demands both speed and athleticism.

In Agility, the dog completes an obstacle course, which includes jumps, tunnels, weaving poles and contact equipment (A-frame, dog-walk and seesaw), under the guidance of his owner.

You need a good element of control, as the dog is working off-lead.

In competition, each dog completes the course individually and is assessed on both time and accuracy. The dog that completes the course with the fewest faults, in the fastest time, wins the class.

A Greyhound certainly has the pace for agility and he is a natural jumper.

He will find some of the obstacles hard to negotiate, such as dipping down to enter tunnels, and working through the weaving poles, but a number of Greyhounds have achieved a high degree of success in this sport.

Therapy dogs

The Greyhound is one of the most gentle of all breeds, and this makes him an ideal candidate for therapy work. It is now well documented that interacting with a dog has great benefits.

The act of stroking and talking to a dog is calming and can help those who are frail, recovering from illness, or those with mental health issues.

There are various organisations that run schemes where dogs and their owners visit hospitals, care homes, schools and other long-stay institutions.

For your Greyhound to qualify for therapy work he will have to undergo temperament testing and carry out a few basic exercises to ensure he is calm and well-behaved in all situations.

Greyhounds can make wonderful therapy dogs.

|Health care

We are fortunate that the Greyhound is a healthy breed and with good routine care, a well-balanced diet, and sufficient exercise, most will experience few health problems.

Vaccinations

Dogs are subject to a number of contagious diseases. In the old days, these were killers, and resulted in heartbreak for many owners. Vaccinations have now been developed, and the occurrence of the major infectious diseases is now very rare.

However, this will only remain the case if all pet owners follow a strict policy of vaccinating their dogs.

There are vaccinations available for the following diseases:

Adenovirus (Canine Adenovirus): This attacks the liver and affected dogs have a classic 'blue eye'.

Distemper: A viral disease which causes chest and gastro-intestinal damage. The brain may also be affected, leading to fits and paralysis.

Parvovirus: Causes severe gastro enteritis, and most commonly affects puppies.

Leptospirosis: This bacterial disease is carried by rats and affects many mammals, including humans. It causes liver and kidney damage.

Rabies: A virus that affects the nervous system and is invariably fatal. The first signs are abnormal behaviour when the infected dog may bite another animal or a person. Paralysis and death follow. Vaccination is compulsory in most countries. In the UK, dogs travelling overseas must be vaccinated.

Kennel cough: There are several strains of kennel cough, but they all result in a harsh, dry, cough. This disease is rarely fatal; in fact most dogs make a good recovery within a matter of weeks and show few signs of ill health while they are affected. However, kennel cough is highly infectious among dogs that live together so, for this reason, most boarding kennels will insist that your dog is protected by the vaccine, which is given as nose drops.

Lyme disease: This is a bacterial disease transmitted by ticks. The first signs are limping, but the heart, kidneys and nervous system can also be affected. The ticks that transmit the disease occur in specific regions, such as the north-east states of the USA, some of the southern states, California and the upper Mississippi region.

Lyme disease is still rare in the UK so vaccinations are not routinely offered.

Vaccination programme

In the USA, the American Animal Hospital Association advises vaccination for core diseases, which they list as distemper, adenovirus, parvovirus and rabies.

The requirement for vaccinating for non-core diseases – leptospriosis, Lyme disease and kennel cough – should be assessed depending on a dog's individual risk and his likely exposure to the disease.

In the UK, vaccinations are routinely given for distemper, adenovirus, leptospirosis and parvovirus.

In most cases, a puppy will start his vaccinations at around eight weeks of age, with the second part given a fortnight later. However, this does vary depending on the individual policy of veterinary practices, and the incidence of disease in your area.

You should also talk to your vet about whether to

give annual booster vaccinations. This depends on an individual dog's levels of immunity, and how long a particular vaccine remains effective.

Parasites

No matter how well you look after your Greyhound, you will have to accept that parasites (internal and external) are ever present, and you need to take preventative action.

Internal parasites: As the name suggests, these parasites live inside your dog. Most will find a home in the digestive tract, but there is also a parasite that lives in the heart. If infestation is unchecked, a dog's health will be severely jeopardised, but routine preventative treatment is simple and effective.

External parasites: These parasites live on your dog's body – in his skin and fur, and sometimes in his ears.

Roundworm

This is found in the small intestine, and signs of infestation will be a poor coat, a pot belly, diarrhoea and lethargy. Pregnant mothers should be treated, but it is almost inevitable that parasites will be passed on to the puppies.

For this reason, a breeder will start a worming

programme, which you will need to continue. Ask your vet for advice on treatment, which will be ongoing throughout your dog's life.

Tapeworm

Infection occurs when fleas and lice are ingested; the adult worm takes up residence in the small intestine, releasing mobile segments (which contain eggs) that can be seen in a dog's faeces as small rice-like grains. The only other obvious sign of infestation is irritation of the anus. Again, routine preventative treatment is required throughout your Greyhound's life.

Heartworm

This parasite is transmitted by mosquitoes, and so will only occur where these insects thrive. A warm environment is needed for the parasite to develop, so it is more likely to be present in areas with a warm, humid climate. However, it is found in all parts of the USA, although its prevalence does vary. At present, heartworm is rarely seen in the UK.

Heartworm live in the right side of the heart. Larvae can grow up to 14 inches (35.5cm) in length.

A dog with heartworm is at severe risk from heart failure, so preventative treatment, as advised by your vet, is essential. Dogs living in the USA should have regular blood tests to check for the presence of infection.

Lungworm

Lungworm, or *Angiostrongylus vasorum*, is a parasite that lives in the heart and major blood vessels supplying the lungs. It can cause many problems, such as breathing difficulties, blood-clotting, sickness and diarrhoea, seizures, and can be fatal.

The parasite is carried by slugs and snails, and the dog becomes infected when ingesting these, often accidentally when rummaging through undergrowth.

Lungworm is not common, but it is on the increase and a responsible owner should be aware of it.

Fortunately, it is easily preventable and even affected dogs usually make a full recovery if treated early enough. Your vet will be able to advise you on the risks in your area and what form of treatment may be required.

Fleas

A dog may carry dog fleas, cat fleas, and even human fleas. The flea stays on the dog only long enough to have a blood meal and to breed, but its presence will result in itching and scratching.

If your dog has an allergy to fleas, which is usually a reaction to the flea's saliva, he will scratch himself until he is raw.

There are a number of treatments available including spot-on treatment, insecticidal shampoo, insecticidal spray and oral medication.

Ask your vet to explain the benefits of the products so you can make an informed choice.

Bear in mind that the whole environment your dog lives in will need to be sprayed, and all other pets living in your home will also need to be treated.

How to detect fleas

You may suspect your dog has fleas, but how can you be sure? There are two methods to try.

Run a fine comb through your dog's coat, and see if you can detect the presence of fleas on the skin, or clinging to the comb. Alternatively, sit your dog on white paper and rub his back. This will dislodge faeces from the fleas, which will be visible as small brown specks. To double check, shake the specks on to damp cotton-wool. Flea faeces consists of the dried blood taken from the host, so if the specks turn a lighter shade of red, you know your dog has fleas.

Ticks

These are blood-sucking parasites which are most frequently found in rural areas where sheep or deer are present.

The main danger is their ability to pass Lyme disease to both dogs and humans. Lyme disease is prevalent in some areas of the USA, although it is still rare in the UK.

The treatment you give your dog for fleas generally works for ticks, but you should discuss the best product to use with your vet.

How to remove a tick

If you spot a tick on your dog, do not try to pluck it off as you risk leaving the hard mouth parts embedded in his skin. The best way to remove a tick is to use a fine pair of tweezers, or you can buy a tick remover. Grasp the tick head firmly and then pull the tick straight out from the skin. If you are using a tick remover, check the instructions, as some recommend a circular twist when pulling. When you have removed the tick, clean the area with mild soap and water.

Ear mites

These parasites live in the outer ear canal. The signs of infestation are a brown, waxy discharge, and your dog will continually shake his head and scratch his ear.

If you suspect your Greyhound has ear mites, a visit to the vet will be needed so that medicated ear drops can be prescribed.

Fur mites

These small, white parasites are visible to the naked eye and are often referred to as 'walking dandruff'.

They cause a scurfy coat and mild itchiness. However, they are zoonetic – transferable to humans – so prompt treatment with an insecticide prescribed by your vet is essential.

Harvest mites

These are picked up from the undergrowth, and can be seen as a bright orange patch on the webbing between the toes, although this can be found elsewhere on the body, such as on the ears flaps. Treatment is effective with the appropriate insecticide.

Skin mites

There are two types of parasite that burrow into a dog's skin. *Demodex canis* is transferred from a mother to her pups while they are feeding.

Treatment is with a topical preparation, and sometimes antibiotics are needed.

The other skin mite, *Sarcoptes scabiei*, causes intense itching and hair loss. It is highly contagious, so all dogs in a household will need to be treated, which involves repeated bathing with a medicated shampoo.

Common ailments

As with all living animals, dogs can be affected by a variety of ailments. Most can be treated effectively after consulting with your vet, who will prescribe appropriate medication and will advise you on how to meet your dog's needs.

Here are some of the more common problems that could affect your Greyhound, with advice on how to deal with them.

Anal glands

These are two small sacs on either side of the anus, which produce a dark-brown secretion that dogs use when they mark their territory. The anal glands should empty every time a dog defecates but if they become blocked or impacted, a dog will experience increasing discomfort. He may nibble at his rear end,

or scoot his bottom along the ground to relieve the irritation. Treatment involves a trip to the vet, who will empty the glands manually. It is important to do this without delay or infection may occur.

Dental problems

Good dental hygiene will do much to minimise gum infection and tooth decay, which is why teeth cleaning should be part of your regular care routine. If tartar accumulates to the extent that you cannot remove it by brushing, the vet will need to intervene. In a situation such as this, an anaesthetic will need to be administered so the tartar can be removed manually.

Diarrhoea

There are many reasons why a dog has diarrhoea, but most commonly it is the result of scavenging, a sudden change of diet, or an adverse reaction to a particular type of food.

If your dog is suffering from diarrhoea, the first step is to withdraw food for a day. It is important that he does not dehydrate, so make sure that fresh drinking water is available. However, drinking too much can increase the diarrhoea, which may be accompanied by vomiting, so limit how much he drinks at any one time.

After allowing the stomach to rest, feed a bland diet, such as white fish or chicken with boiled rice, for a few days. In most cases, your dog's motions will return to normal and you can resume usual feeding, although this should be done gradually.

However, if this fails to work and the diarrhoea persists for more than a few days, you should consult you vet. Your dog may have an infection which needs to be treated with antibiotics, or the diarrhoea may indicate some other problem which needs expert diagnosis.

Ear infections

The Greyhound has rose-shaped ears which are semi-pricked when he is alert. This allows air to circulate reasonably freely which helps to prevent infection. A healthy ear is clean with no sign of redness or inflammation, and no evidence of a waxy brown discharge or a foul odour. If you see your dog scratching his ear, shaking his head, or holding one ear at an odd angle, you will need to consult your vet.

The most likely causes are ear mites, an infection, or there may be a foreign body, such as a grass seed, trapped in the ear. Depending on the cause, treatment is with medicated ear drops, possibly containing antibiotics. If a foreign body is suspected, the vet will need to carry our further investigations.

Eye problems

The Greyhound has oval-shaped eyes which are neither sunken nor prominent. This lack of exaggeration means that his eyes are not predisposed to infection or vulnerable to injury or trauma, which is the case with breeds such as the Pekingese, that have somewhat bulging eyes.

However, if your Greyhound's eyes look red and sore, he may be suffering from conjunctivitis. This may, or may not be accompanied with a watery or a crusty discharge. Conjunctivitis can be caused by a bacterial or viral infection, it could be the result of an injury, or it could be an adverse reaction to pollen.

You will need to consult your vet for a correct diagnosis, but in the case of an infection, treatment with medicated eye drops is effective.

Foreign bodies

Regardless of age, there are some Greyhounds who cannot resist chewing anything that looks interesting. The toys you choose for your dog should be suitably robust to withstand damage, but children's toys can be irresistible. Some dogs will chew – and swallow – anything from socks, tights, and any other items from the laundry basket to golf balls and stones from the garden. Obviously,

these items are indigestible and could cause an obstruction in your dog's intestine, which is potentially lethal.

The signs to look for are vomiting, and a tucked up posture. The dog will often be restless and will look as though he is in pain. In this situation, you must get your dog to the vet without delay, as surgery may be needed to remove the obstruction.

Heatstroke

The Greyhound is built for speed and an efficient respiratory system is, therefore, of paramount importance. However, he carries very little body fat and this makes him vulnerable to extremes of temperature – suffering from the cold or over-heating.

It is easy to cope with cold conditions by keeping the house warm and fitting your Greyhound with a jacket when he goes out, but dealing with the effects of higher temperatures can be problematic. A Greyhound does not need to be exposed to soaring temperatures to suffer from heatstroke, it can happen on a moderately warm day if you are not being vigilant. If the weather is warm, make sure your Greyhound has access to shady areas, and wait for a cooler part of the day before going for a walk.

Be extra careful if you leave your Greyhound in the car as the temperature can rise dramatically – even on a cloudy day. Heatstroke can happen very rapidly, and unless you are able lower your dog's temperature, it can be fatal.

If your dog appears to be suffering from heatstroke, lie him flat and work at lowering his temperature by spraying him with cool water and covering him with wet towels. As soon as he has made some recovery, take him to the vet, where cold intravenous fluids can be administered.

Lameness/ limping

There are a wide variety of reasons why a dog can go lame, from a simple muscle strain, to a fracture, ligament damage, or more complex problems with the joints. If you are concerned about your dog, do not delay in seeking help. As your Greyhound becomes more elderly, he may suffer from arthritis, which you will see as general stiffness, particularly when he gets up after resting. This may well be the case if your Greyhound has suffered an injury during his racing career. It will help if you ensure his bed is in a warm draught-free location, and if he gets wet after exercise, you must dry him thoroughly. If your Greyhound seems to be in pain, consult your vet who will be able to help with pain relief medication.

Skin problems

If your dog is scratching or nibbling at his skin, first check he is free from fleas. There are other external parasites which cause itching and hair loss, but you will need a vet to help you find the culprit. An allergic reaction is another major cause of skin problems. It can be quite an undertaking to find the cause of the allergy, and you will need to follow your vet's advice, which often requires eliminating specific ingredients from the diet, as well as looking at environmental factors.

Breed-specific disorders

Like all pedigree dogs, the Greyhound does have some breed-related disorders, although they are few in number. If diagnosed with any of the diseases listed here, it is important to remember that they can affect offspring so breeding from such dogs should be discouraged.

There are now recognised screening tests to enable breeders to check for affected individuals and hence reduce the prevalence of these diseases within the breed.

DNA testing is also becoming more widely available, and as research into the different genetic diseases progresses, more DNA tests are being developed.

Cancer

Osteosarcoma

This form of cancer may affect the forelimbs and, less commonly, the femur. It is more likely to occur in middle-aged Greyhounds and may spread to other sites, particularly the lungs.

Congenital deafness

This is associated with the piebald gene and an increased proportion of white coat colouring. Hearing appears to be normal at birth but deteriorates from around four weeks. BAER testing, at five week,s will give an accurate diagnosis.

Eye disorders

Pannus

This is a long-term inflammation of the cornea, often accompanied by conjunctivitis. The degree of the problem varies but it can result in blindness.

Treatment involves limiting the effects of the inflammation and minimising exposure to the ultra violet effects of the sun. Onset is around two to five years of age.

Progressive retinal atrophy

This is a condition which involves the destruction of the photoreceptors in the retina. As the disease progresses the retina shrivels up, resulting in total loss of vision. Onset is generally around 12 months of age.

Skin disorders

Cutaneous asthenia

Also known as Ehler-Danos syndrome, this results in an unusually stretchy skin which is prone to tearing. The tears, often cased by scratching, may heal as small white scars or, in more severe cases, they may need to be stitched. The joints and eyes may also be affected.

Idiopathic cutaneous and renal glomerular vasculopathy

Signs may appear as early as six months or as late as five years of age. The hocks, stifles and inner thighs become swollen and tender; in some cases the forelimbs are also affected. Deep ulceration may occur and if the kidney becomes diseased, the condition may be fatal. Skin biopsies are needed for an accurate diagnosis.

Pattern baldness

This is more likely to affect bitches. It involves fur loss from the temples, the underside of the neck, chest and abdomen. There is no discomfort but there is no treatment to reverse the baldness.

Summing up

It may give the pet owner cause for concern to find out about health problems that may affect their dog. But it is important to bear in mind that acquiring some basic knowledge is an asset, as it will allow you to spot signs of trouble at an early stage.

Early diagnosis is very often the means to the most effective treatment. Fortunately, the Greyhound is a generally healthy and disease-free dog, with his only visits to the vet being annual check-ups.

In most cases, owners can look forward to enjoying many happy years with this affectionate and highly

Useful addresses

Breed & Kennel Clubs

Please contact your Kennel Club to obtain contact information about breed clubs in your area.

UK

The Kennel Club (UK)
1 Clarges Street London, W1J 8AB
Telephone: 0870 606 6750
Fax: 0207 518 1058
Web: www.thekennelclub.org.uk

USA

American Kennel Club (AKC)
5580 Centerview Drive, Raleigh, NC 27606.
Telephone: 919 233 9767
Fax: 919 233 3627
Email: info@akc.org
Web: www.akc.org

United Kennel Club (UKC)
100 E Kilgore Rd, Kalamazoo,
MI 49002-5584, USA.
Tel: 269 343 9020
Fax: 269 343 7037
Web: www.ukcdogs.com/

Australia

Australian National Kennel Council (ANKC)
The Australian National Kennel Council is the administrative body for pure breed canine affairs in Australia. It does not, however, deal directly with dog exhibitors, breeders or judges. For information pertaining to breeders, clubs or shows, please contact the relevant State or Territory Body.

International

Fédération Cynologique Internationalé (FCI)
Place Albert 1er, 13, B-6530 Thuin, Belgium.
Tel: +32 71 59.12.38
Fax: +32 71 59.22.29
Web: www.fci.be/

Training and behavior

UK

Association of Pet Dog Trainers
Telephone: 01285 810811
Web: www.apdt.co.uk

Canine Behaviour
Association of Pet Behaviour Counsellors
Telephone: 01386 751151
Web: www.apbc.org.uk/

USA

Association of Pet Dog Trainers
Tel: 1 800 738 3647
Web: www.apdt.com/

American College of Veterinary Behaviorists
Web: dacvb.org/

American Veterinary Society of Animal Behavior
Web: www.avsabonline.org/

Australia

APDT Australia Inc
Web: www.apdt.com.au

For details of regional behaviorists, contact the relevant State or Territory Controlling Body.

Activities

UK

Agility Club
www.agilityclub.co.uk/

British Flyball Association
Telephone: 01628 829623
Web: www.flyball.org.uk/

USA

North American Dog Agility Council
Web: www.nadac.com/

North American Flyball Association, Inc.
Tel/Fax: 800 318 6312
Web: www.flyball.org/

Australia

Agility Dog Association of Australia
Tel: 0423 138 914
Web: www.adaa.com.au/

NADAC Australia
Web: www.nadacaustralia.com/

Australian Flyball Association
Tel: 0407 337 939
Web: www.flyball.org.au/

International

World Canine Freestyle Organisation
Tel: (718) 332-8336
Web: www.worldcaninefreestyle.org

Health

UK

British Small Animal Veterinary Association
Tel: 01452 726700
Web: www.bsava.com/

Royal College of Veterinary Surgeons
Tel: 0207 222 2001
Web: www.rcvs.org.uk

Alternative Veterinary Medicine Centre
Tel: 01367 710324
Web: www.alternativevet.org/

USA

American Veterinary Medical Association
Tel: 800 248 2862
Web: www.avma.org

American College of Veterinary Surgeons
Tel: 301 916 0200
Toll Free: 877 217 2287
Web: www.acvs.org/

Canine Eye Registration Foundation
The Veterinary Medical DataBases
1717 Philo Rd, PO Box 3007,
Urbana, IL 61803-3007
Tel: 217-693-4800
Fax: 217-693-4801
Web: www.vmdb.org/cerf.html

Orthopaedic Foundation of Animals
2300 E Nifong Boulevard
Columbia, Missouri, 65201-3806
Tel: 573 442-0418
Fax: 573 875-5073
Web: www.offa.org/

American Holistic Veterinary Medical
Association
Tel: 410 569 0795
Web: www.ahvma.org/

Australia

Australian Small Animal Veterinary
Association
Tel: 02 9431 5090
Web: www.asava.com.au

Australian Veterinary Association
Tel: 02 9431 5000
Web: www.ava.com.au

Australian College Veterinary Scientists
Tel: 07 3423 2016
Web: acvsc.org.au

Australian Holistic Vets
Web: www.ahv.com.au/